EMMANUEL JOSEPH

Empires Without Borders, How Billionaires Shape Nations and Redefine Global Power

Copyright © 2025 by Emmanuel Joseph

All rights reserved. No part of this publication may be reproduced, stored or transmitted in any form or by any means, electronic, mechanical, photocopying, recording, scanning, or otherwise without written permission from the publisher. It is illegal to copy this book, post it to a website, or distribute it by any other means without permission.

First edition

This book was professionally typeset on Reedsy.
Find out more at reedsy.com

Contents

1	Chapter 1: The Rise of the Global Billionaire	1
2	Chapter 2: The Wealth Gap	3
3	Chapter 3: Philanthropy and Influence	5
4	Chapter 4: Political Power and Lobbying	7
5	Chapter 5: Media Ownership and Control	9
6	Chapter 6: The Tech Titans	11
7	Chapter 7: Global Real Estate Empires	13
8	Chapter 8: The Art of Tax Avoidance	15
9	Chapter 9: The Global Workforce	17
10	Chapter 10: Environmental Impact and Sustainability	19
11	Chapter 11: Innovation and Risk-Taking	21
12	Chapter 12: The Global Financial System	23
13	Chapter 13: Education and Knowledge	25
14	Chapter 14: Health and Medicine	27
15	Chapter 15: Culture and Entertainment	29
16	Chapter 16: The Global Economy	31
17	Chapter 17: The Ethical and Moral Debate	33

1

Chapter 1: The Rise of the Global Billionaire

The phenomenon of the global billionaire has become increasingly prominent over the past few decades. These ultra-wealthy individuals not only amass immense fortunes but also wield significant influence over global affairs. From technological innovation to political lobbying, the reach of billionaires extends far beyond their bank accounts. This chapter explores the origins and rise of global billionaires, shedding light on their impact on society and the world.

Historically, wealth accumulation has always played a crucial role in shaping societies. From the powerful monarchs of ancient civilizations to the industrial magnates of the 19th century, those with substantial wealth have often driven progress and change. In modern times, the rise of global billionaires can be traced back to the rapid advancements in technology and the interconnectedness brought about by globalization. This new breed of wealthy individuals has leveraged these factors to amass fortunes that dwarf those of their predecessors.

The role of technology and globalization in creating opportunities for massive wealth generation cannot be overstated. The digital revolution has given birth to entirely new industries, such as e-commerce, social media, and fintech, which have produced some of the wealthiest individuals in history. Moreover, globalization has opened up new markets and allowed for unprecedented levels of international trade and investment. This combination of technological innovation and global interconnectedness has created a fertile ground for the rise of global billionaires.

Case studies of notable billionaires provide insight into their early ventures and the strategies they employed to build their empires. For example, Jeff Bezos, the founder of Amazon, started his journey by selling books online from his garage. Elon Musk, the visionary behind companies like Tesla and SpaceX, faced numerous setbacks before achieving success. These stories highlight the entrepreneurial spirit, risk-taking, and innovation that characterize many of today's billionaires. By examining their paths to success, we can better understand the factors that contribute to the rise of global billionaires.

2

Chapter 2: The Wealth Gap

The wealth gap between the rich and the poor has been a topic of growing concern in recent years. As billionaires accumulate vast fortunes, the disparity between the wealthy and the less fortunate continues to widen. This chapter examines the factors contributing to the wealth gap and its impact on social stability and economic growth.

Several factors contribute to the growing wealth gap, including economic policies, globalization, and technological advancements. Economic policies that favor the wealthy, such as tax cuts for high-income individuals and deregulation of industries, can exacerbate income inequality. Globalization has also played a role, as it has allowed multinational corporations to maximize profits by outsourcing labor to countries with lower wages. Additionally, technological advancements have led to the automation of jobs, resulting in job displacement and wage stagnation for many workers.

The impact of the wealth gap on social stability and economic growth is profound. High levels of income inequality can lead to social unrest, as people become increasingly frustrated with their lack of economic opportunities. Moreover, the concentration of wealth in the hands of a few can stifle economic growth, as it reduces the purchasing power of the majority. This chapter delves into the consequences of the wealth gap and the ways it affects society as a whole.

Efforts to address the wealth gap have been met with varying degrees of success. Some countries have implemented progressive tax policies, increased social spending, and introduced measures to protect workers' rights. However, these efforts are often met with resistance from powerful interests that benefit from the status quo. By examining the effectiveness of these initiatives, we can better understand the challenges and potential solutions for closing the wealth gap.

3

Chapter 3: Philanthropy and Influence

Billionaire philanthropy has become a defining feature of modern society. While some view it as a noble endeavor to address social and economic inequalities, others see it as a means for the wealthy to exert control and influence over public policy. This chapter explores the role of billionaire philanthropy in shaping societal outcomes and the ethical considerations it raises.

Major philanthropic efforts by billionaires have had significant impacts on various sectors, from education and healthcare to environmental conservation and social justice. For instance, the Bill and Melinda Gates Foundation has invested billions in global health initiatives, eradicating diseases and improving access to vaccines. Similarly, Warren Buffett's substantial donations to charitable causes have supported numerous social programs. These case studies illustrate the positive contributions of billionaire philanthropy.

However, the debate over whether philanthropy is a form of influence and control is ongoing. Critics argue that billionaire philanthropy allows the wealthy to set agendas and priorities based on their interests rather than public needs. This can lead to a concentration of power in the hands of a few individuals, potentially undermining democratic processes and public accountability.

The ethical considerations and criticisms of billionaire philanthropy are multifaceted. While some argue that the wealthy have a moral obligation to give back to society, others contend that philanthropy can perpetuate systemic inequalities by allowing billionaires to maintain their power and influence. This chapter delves into these ethical dilemmas, exploring the balance between philanthropy and social responsibility.

4

Chapter 4: Political Power and Lobbying

Billionaires wield considerable political power through their financial resources and ability to influence public policy. This chapter examines how billionaires use their wealth to shape political outcomes, including the mechanics of lobbying and campaign financing.

Political lobbying and campaign financing are key tools billionaires use to exert their influence. By funding political campaigns, they can gain access to policymakers and push for legislation that aligns with their interests. This often involves hiring lobbyists to advocate on their behalf and contribute to political action committees (PACs) that support their preferred candidates.

Case studies of billionaires who have successfully influenced political decisions highlight the extent of their power. For example, the Koch brothers have spent millions on political campaigns and advocacy groups to promote conservative policies. Similarly, George Soros has funded numerous progressive initiatives and candidates through his Open Society Foundations. These examples demonstrate how billionaires can shape political landscapes.

The implications of concentrated political power in the hands of a few are profound. It raises concerns about the erosion of democratic principles and the potential for policy decisions to favor the wealthy at the expense of the broader population. This chapter explores the impact of billionaire influence on political processes and the challenges it poses to democracy.

5

Chapter 5: Media Ownership and Control

The acquisition of media companies by billionaires has significant implications for information dissemination and public opinion. This chapter explores the impact of billionaire-owned media on shaping narratives and controlling the flow of information.

Media plays a crucial role in shaping public opinion and policy by influencing how information is presented and perceived. Billionaire ownership of media outlets can lead to biased reporting and agenda-setting that aligns with the owner's interests. This concentration of media power raises concerns about the integrity of journalism and the diversity of viewpoints.

Case studies of media moguls, such as Rupert Murdoch and Jeff Bezos, illustrate the influence of billionaire-owned media. Murdoch's ownership of News Corp, which includes outlets like Fox News and The Wall Street Journal, has had a significant impact on political discourse and public opinion. Bezos's acquisition of The Washington Post has also sparked debates about the independence of journalism and potential conflicts of interest.

The ethical implications of media ownership and control by billionaires are complex. While some argue that wealthy individuals can provide the necessary resources to sustain quality journalism, others contend that it undermines the principles of free and independent media. This chapter delves into these ethical considerations and the broader impact of billionaire-owned media on society.

6

Chapter 6: The Tech Titans

Tech billionaires have emerged as some of the most influential figures in the global economy. This chapter examines the rise of tech titans and their impact on industries, innovation, and society.

The digital revolution has given birth to tech giants who have redefined entire industries. Companies like Apple, Google, Facebook, and Microsoft have not only transformed how we live and work but also created immense wealth for their founders. The role of innovation and disruption in creating tech wealth is a defining feature of this new era.

Case studies of tech giants, such as Steve Jobs, Mark Zuckerberg, and Larry Page, illustrate their global influence. Jobs's vision for Apple revolutionized the technology industry and consumer electronics. Zuckerberg's creation of Facebook changed the way people communicate and share information. Page's contributions to Google's search engine and other innovations have had a profound impact on the internet and digital services.

The future of technology holds the potential for further concentration of wealth and influence among tech billionaires. As emerging technologies like artificial intelligence, blockchain, and quantum computing continue to develop, the dominance of tech titans is likely to expand. This chapter explores the implications of this trend and the potential challenges it presents for society.

7

Chapter 7: Global Real Estate Empires

The accumulation of vast real estate holdings by billionaires around the world has significant economic and social implications. This chapter examines the impact of billionaire-owned real estate on local economies and communities.

Billionaire-owned real estate can shape local economies by driving up property values and altering the character of neighborhoods. This can lead to gentrification, displacing long-time residents and changing the socio-economic landscape. The impact on local businesses and communities can be profound, as rising rents and property prices make it difficult for small businesses and lower-income residents to thrive.

Case studies of real estate tycoons, such as Donald Trump and Li Ka-shing, illustrate their vast portfolios and influence. Trump's real estate empire includes iconic properties like Trump Tower and numerous luxury hotels and golf courses. Li Ka-shing's holdings span across multiple countries, with investments in commercial, residential, and infrastructure properties. These examples highlight the global reach and power of real estate billionaires.

The ethical and social implications of massive real estate ownership by billionaires are complex. While their investments can drive economic development and create jobs, they can also exacerbate inequality and contribute to social tensions. This chapter explores these dynamics and the challenges of balancing economic growth with social responsibility.

8

Chapter 8: The Art of Tax Avoidance

Tax avoidance strategies employed by billionaires have become a topic of intense scrutiny and debate. This chapter explores the methods used by the ultra-wealthy to minimize their tax liabilities and the broader implications of these practices.

Billionaires use various strategies to reduce their tax burdens, including offshore accounts, tax shelters, and complex financial arrangements. By leveraging legal loopholes and sophisticated tax planning, they can significantly lower their effective tax rates. These strategies often involve the use of trusts, shell companies, and charitable foundations to shield income and assets from taxation.

Case studies of tax avoidance schemes provide insight into their mechanics and legal implications. For instance, the Paradise Papers and Panama Papers leaks revealed the extent to which wealthy individuals and corporations go to minimize their tax liabilities. These revelations have sparked public outrage and calls for greater transparency and accountability in the global financial system.

Efforts to reform tax policies and address tax avoidance have faced significant challenges. Governments around the world have implemented measures to close loopholes and increase tax enforcement, but these efforts are often met with resistance from powerful interests. This chapter examines the effectiveness of these reforms and the ongoing battle to ensure a fairer tax system.

9

Chapter 9: The Global Workforce

Billionaires play a crucial role in shaping global labor markets through their investments and business practices. This chapter examines the impact of outsourcing, automation, and labor policies on employment and working conditions.

Outsourcing and automation have become key strategies for billionaires looking to maximize profits and efficiency. By relocating production to countries with lower labor costs and investing in automated technologies, companies can reduce expenses and increase productivity. However, these practices often lead to job displacement and wage stagnation for workers in higher-cost countries.

Case studies of companies with significant billionaire influence, such as Apple, Amazon, and Walmart, illustrate the impact of their labor practices on the global workforce. Apple's reliance on overseas manufacturing, Amazon's use of warehouse automation, and Walmart's labor policies have all had profound effects on employment and working conditions.

The future of work in a billionaire-dominated economy raises important questions about the balance between economic growth and worker well-being. As technological advancements continue to reshape labor markets, it is essential to consider policies that protect workers' rights and ensure equitable distribution of the benefits of economic progress. This chapter explores potential solutions and the challenges of creating a fairer labor market.

10

Chapter 10: Environmental Impact and Sustainability

The environmental footprint of billionaire-owned businesses is a critical issue in the debate over sustainable development. This chapter examines the impact of these enterprises on the environment and the role of billionaires in promoting or hindering sustainability efforts.

Billionaire-owned businesses often have significant environmental impacts due to their scale and resource consumption. Industries such as fossil fuels, mining, and manufacturing are major contributors to pollution and environmental degradation. The practices of these companies can have far-reaching consequences for ecosystems and communities.

Case studies of environmental initiatives led by billionaires, such as Elon Musk's push for renewable energy with Tesla and SpaceX, and Jeff Bezos's investment in climate change mitigation through the Bezos Earth Fund, highlight the potential for positive contributions. These initiatives demonstrate how billionaires can leverage their resources to address pressing environmental challenges.

The balance between economic growth and environmental responsibility is a complex and often contentious issue. While some billionaires are committed to sustainable practices, others prioritize profit over environmental protection. This chapter explores the ethical considerations and potential solutions for achieving a more sustainable future in a billionaire-driven world.

11

Chapter 11: Innovation and Risk-Taking

Billionaires are often at the forefront of innovation and risk-taking, driving progress in various industries. This chapter examines the role of billionaire-funded ventures in shaping the future and the impact of their risk-taking on society.

Innovation and disruption are key characteristics of many billionaire entrepreneurs. By investing in cutting-edge technologies and exploring new business models, they create opportunities for economic growth and societal advancement. The willingness to take risks and embrace uncertainty is a defining trait of successful billionaires.

Case studies of innovative projects, such as Elon Musk's SpaceX and Tesla, Richard Branson's Virgin Galactic, and Jeff Bezos's Blue Origin, illustrate the transformative potential of billionaire-funded ventures. These projects not only push the boundaries of what is possible but also inspire a new generation of entrepreneurs and innovators.

The future of innovation in a billionaire-driven world holds immense potential but also raises important questions about the distribution of benefits and risks. While billionaire-funded ventures can drive progress, they can also exacerbate inequalities and create new challenges. This chapter explores the implications of innovation and risk-taking for society and the potential paths forward.

12

Chapter 12: The Global Financial System

Billionaires exert significant influence on the global financial system through their investments and ownership of financial institutions. This chapter examines the impact of their financial activities on global markets and economies.

Billionaire-owned financial institutions and investment firms play a crucial role in shaping global economic trends. By directing vast amounts of capital, they can influence market dynamics, drive investment flows, and shape economic policies. Their decisions have far-reaching consequences for businesses, governments, and individuals.

Case studies of financial crises, such as the 2008 global financial meltdown, highlight the role of billionaire investors and financial institutions in both causing and mitigating economic downturns. Figures like Warren Buffett and George Soros have been pivotal in navigating financial markets and influencing economic policies during times of crisis.

The implications of concentrated financial power are significant, raising questions about accountability, transparency, and the potential for systemic risks. This chapter explores the challenges of regulating billionaire-owned financial institutions and ensuring a stable and equitable global financial system.

13

Chapter 13: Education and Knowledge

Billionaire-funded education initiatives have a profound impact on global knowledge dissemination and educational access. This chapter examines the role of private funding in shaping educational institutions and curricula.

Private funding by billionaires can transform educational institutions by providing resources for research, scholarships, and infrastructure. Initiatives like the Chan Zuckerberg Initiative and the Bill and Melinda Gates Foundation have invested heavily in education, aiming to improve access and outcomes for students around the world.

Case studies of educational philanthropists and their projects, such as Laurene Powell Jobs's support for innovative schools and Michael Bloomberg's investment in public education, highlight the potential for positive change. These initiatives demonstrate how private funding can address gaps in public education systems and drive educational innovation.

The ethical considerations of private influence on education are complex, raising questions about equity, accountability, and the potential for agenda-setting. This chapter explores the balance between private funding and public oversight in ensuring that educational initiatives serve the broader public interest.

14

Chapter 14: Health and Medicine

Billionaires have a significant impact on the global health and medical industries through their investments and philanthropic efforts. This chapter examines their role in driving medical research, innovation, and access to healthcare.

Private funding by billionaires has the potential to accelerate medical research and innovation. Investments in biotech startups, healthcare facilities, and research institutions can lead to breakthroughs in treatments and technologies. The contributions of billionaires like Bill Gates in fighting infectious diseases and funding vaccine research are notable examples.

Case studies of health initiatives led by billionaires, such as the Wellcome Trust and the Howard Hughes Medical Institute, illustrate the transformative potential of private funding in healthcare. These initiatives have driven significant advancements in medical science and improved access to healthcare for underserved populations.

The future of healthcare in a billionaire-influenced world raises important questions about equity, access, and the role of private interests in public health. This chapter explores the ethical considerations and potential solutions for ensuring that healthcare innovations benefit all members of society.

15

Chapter 15: Culture and Entertainment

The impact of billionaire-owned entertainment and cultural enterprises on global culture is significant. This chapter examines how billionaires shape cultural trends and artistic expression through their investments and ownership of media, entertainment, and arts institutions.

Private funding from billionaires can drive the production of movies, television shows, and music, influencing cultural trends and public perceptions. Their ownership of entertainment companies allows them to shape content and narratives, often reflecting their personal values and interests. This control over cultural production can have far-reaching effects on societal norms and values.

Case studies of cultural and entertainment moguls, such as Walt Disney, David Geffen, and Jay-Z, highlight their influence on global culture. Disney's empire has shaped generations of audiences with its iconic characters and stories. Geffen's contributions to the music industry have launched the careers of countless artists. Jay-Z's ventures in music, fashion, and media have redefined the boundaries of cultural entrepreneurship.

The implications of concentrated cultural influence raise important questions about diversity, representation, and access. While billionaire-owned enterprises can drive innovation and quality, they can also lead to the homogenization of culture and the marginalization of alternative voices. This chapter explores the ethical considerations and potential solutions for ensuring a vibrant and diverse cultural landscape.

16

Chapter 16: The Global Economy

Billionaires have a profound impact on the global economy through their investments, businesses, and philanthropic efforts. This chapter examines their role in shaping economic trends and policies on a global scale.

Billionaire-owned multinational corporations play a significant role in global trade and investment. Their decisions can influence economic policies, labor markets, and supply chains, affecting economies around the world. The scale and reach of these corporations give billionaires substantial power in shaping economic outcomes.

Case studies of economic influence by billionaires, such as Bill Gates, Warren Buffett, and Jack Ma, illustrate their impact on global markets. Gates's investments in technology and philanthropy have driven economic growth and innovation. Buffett's strategic investments through Berkshire Hathaway have influenced various industries. Ma's leadership in e-commerce has transformed retail markets in China and beyond.

The future of the global economy in a billionaire-driven world raises important questions about equity, sustainability, and governance. While billionaires can drive economic progress, their influence also poses challenges related to inequality and market stability. This chapter explores the implications of concentrated economic power and potential paths forward for a more equitable and resilient global economy.

17

Chapter 17: The Ethical and Moral Debate

The ethical and moral considerations of billionaire influence on the world are complex and multifaceted. This chapter examines the debate over wealth accumulation, social responsibility, and the role of regulation in addressing the power of billionaires.

The debate over wealth accumulation and its impact on society is ongoing. Some argue that billionaires have a moral obligation to use their wealth for the greater good, while others contend that extreme wealth concentration perpetuates systemic inequalities. This chapter explores the various perspectives on the ethical implications of wealth accumulation.

The role of regulation and governance in addressing billionaire power is a critical issue. Effective policies and oversight are necessary to ensure that billionaire influence does not undermine democratic principles and public accountability. This chapter examines potential regulatory frameworks and their effectiveness in balancing private interests with public good.

The future of global power dynamics and the role of billionaires will continue to evolve. As societal values and economic systems change, so too will the influence of billionaires. This chapter explores the potential paths forward for a more just and equitable world, where wealth and power are balanced by social responsibility and ethical considerations.

This concludes the book "Empires Without Borders: How Billionaires Shape Nations and Redefine Global Power." I hope you find it engaging and insightful. Is there anything else you'd like to add or modify?

book description

"Empires Without Borders: How Billionaires Shape Nations and Redefine Global Power" is an in-depth exploration of the immense influence wielded by the world's wealthiest individuals. This book delves into the ways billionaires impact our global landscape, from their roles in shaping economies and political systems to their philanthropic efforts and cultural contributions.

Through a series of comprehensive chapters, the book examines the rise of global billionaires and the growing wealth gap, highlighting the social and economic ramifications. It investigates how these ultra-wealthy individuals use their resources to influence political outcomes, control media narratives, and drive technological advancements.

The book also addresses the ethical and moral debates surrounding billionaire power, questioning the balance between private interests and public good. Through detailed case studies and insightful analysis, "Empires Without Borders" provides a nuanced perspective on the complex interplay between wealth, power, and society.

Ultimately, the book seeks to understand the evolving role of billionaires in shaping our world and explores potential paths forward for a more just and equitable future. It is a must-read for anyone interested in the dynamics of global power and the far-reaching impact of the ultra-rich.

www.ingramcontent.com/pod-product-compliance
Lightning Source LLC
LaVergne TN
LVHW020457080526
838202LV00057B/6013